RANDOM
ENCOURAGEMENTS

Finding God in the Everyday

S E Hatfield

Acknowledgements

To my wife Mary, for reading my early manuscripts, sharing honestly, and mostly, for your patience with me while it all came together. Thank you!

To my editor, Linda Bennet, who took random strings of words and turned them into what I was trying to say.

To my good friends over at ChristianWriters.com, thank you for pouring unselfishly into me as a writer.

To Ken Jenkins, whose photography sees God through a lens the way I can only hope to see through a keyboard. Thanks for the Foreword.

To Lynnette Bonner for her amazing cover art.

Finally, I'd like to thank my Lord for allowing me to discover glimpses of His glory in the "everyday."

DEDICATION

This book is dedicated to my mother.

Foreword

We live in a fast-paced world often driven to make a living, and as A.W. Tozer wrote, "We hardly know what that means." All around us, God is working in lives through "simple things" that we often ignore. He has sensitized in a special way some of His desiring children to be able to see with spiritual eyes far deeper than what appears on the surface. That is certainly the case with Stephen Hatfield. He doesn't have to strain to see how God is teaching and touching lives; it is simply a gift that he uses beautifully to open "misty" eyes and to point hearts to see Christ in the midst of every circumstance.

"Random Encouragements" is a breath of fresh air for all of us. Written in the style of a Phillip Keller ("Lessons From A Sheepdog", "A Shepherd Looks At the 23rd Psalm), this book reminds the reader that an omni-present God is always a heartbeat away and that He hears the whispers of our heart. As these experiences cause us to smile and even shed a tear, they also cause us to think and ask, "How do I miss these things in my personal walk with Jesus?"

I am blessed to know Stephen. I watch from afar as he shows a humble kindness to others and a sincere compassion for those who live with a "full plate" while seldom receiving the appreciation they so deserve. He is a servant with much to give and I am thankful that he has shared these windows of beauty with us. We will grow through the pages if we read with hearts wide open and gratitude for the simple things.

Ken Jenkins Heaven's Eyes Ministry Gatlinburg, TN

Table of Contents

Introduction 1

1 The Thrift Store 3

2 The Candle 7

3 The Bowl 11

4 Peas 15

5 The Lake 17

6 The Bow 21

7 The Library 25

8 The Spring 31

9 The Mountain 35

10 The Winter Night Sky 39

11 The Garden 43

12 See the Shot 47

13 Eb and Flo 51

14 The Orchestra 55

15 Beautiful Noise 59

16 Time.. 63

17 New Fallen Snow............................... 67

18 Little Plastic Cup.............................. 71

19 For or With...................................... 75

20 Indiana Corn.................................... 79

21 Fast Food 83

22 The Cardinal 87

23 Hand Crafted 95

Outro.. 98

Introduction

In this fast-paced world we live in, it's easy to get busy and miss the little ways God makes Himself known in our day-to-day lives. This book reflects the truths God has revealed to me in my daily journey.

My hope is you find an ever-present God who speaks to His children through even the most mundane ways.

Random Encouragements: Finding God in the Everyday is a collection of short observations designed to heighten your awareness of God the next time you step out on your porch with a cup of coffee, redecorate your living room, or simply walk into a thrift store. May they be as encouraging to you as they were to me when the Lord gave them.

1

The Thrift Store

Do you ever go shopping at thrift stores? I never did until my wife took me to one in our old hometown. I thought thrift stores were places where folks brought their junk, things stained, torn, broken, or just not needed anymore. Boy was I in for a surprise! Wandering down each aisle, I saw items in different stages of disrepair.

Then something caught my eye. Hanging on the men's rack was an Armani sport coat. I couldn't believe it! Armani! They make nothing cheap. I can't even afford Armani socks. The coat looked brand new and it fit me!

That day I went home with two treasures-the jacket and a lesson learned. I discovered that perceptions can be wrong. Since that experience, I now enjoy hunting treasures with Mary. I've found LL Bean coats, Ralph Lauren shirts, Craftsman tools, and more old books than I dare count. Soon, the hunt became as much fun as the find.

I've also learned persistence. It may take a couple of trips before you find that treasure. You may have to dig deep into the bottom of the bins looking for that special something.

Every item, though discarded for some reason, can be a treasure to someone. What you thought was worthless will be of great value to someone else. It left your world and entered theirs to fulfill their need. Eventually, every item in the thrift store finds a new home. Some items take longer than others for their new owners to find them, but they are all chosen. You see, everyone who enters a thrift store is looking for something.

The world can seem a lot like a thrift store. We can find ourselves gradually used up as we pour ourselves into life. Then one day, we find ourselves cast aside as if we were of no more use, feeling broken by hate or fear, or stained by hurt and pain. Sometimes, through no fault of our own, we're deemed imperfect and find ourselves hanging on a rack in the thrift store.

Then, one morning, the doors to the thrift store open and in He walks, someone who knows a good thing when He sees it, someone who's not afraid to dig deep down in the piles, to flip through all the used magazines. He's not afraid to get His hands dirty searching for a treasure. Suddenly He reaches down, gently wraps His hands around a hurting soul, picks that one up, and smiles as He turns and heads for the door, having found what He was looking for in the bin. On His way out, He passes the checkout counter. Oh, in case you think He's forgetting to stop and pay, Jesus already paid the price for His treasure. He did that about two thousand years ago on a hill called Calvary.

"I praise you because I am fearfully and wonderfully made; your works are wonderful, I know that full well." (Psalm 139:14 NIV)

2

The Candle

My wife decorated our home again yesterday. In the process, she bought another candle. She loves candles, they're in every room and each one is unique. Candles come in all shapes and sizes: round, square, long and thin, from tiny tea lights to big centrepieces.

Watching a candle burn is fascinating. Think about it. As a candle burns, it's not consumed by the flame. It yields itself, softening with the heat of the flame as it moves out of the way, letting the wick burn down to its innermost parts.

Then, there are those wonderful scents: lavender, Christmas tree, gingerbread, ocean breeze, you name it, there's a candle with that scent somewhere. But you can't just read the label. You must light it. Oh, to be sure, you can hold it up close to your nose getting an idea of how it will smell, but only when the flame burns, does the fragrance fill the room.

Even though a candle is designed to burn, we have candles we've never lit in our house. We use them for decoration. But they're still not fulfilling their created purpose. Candles were made to give light, not sit on a shelf or a coffee table.

Did you know darkness can't extinguish light? Darkness only exists when there is no light, and light always chases away darkness.

There was darkness in Gethsemane one night long ago. There, among the olive trees of that garden, was the deepest of darkness. Until, late one night, a Candle walked into that garden. This Candle had the sweetest fragrance. It smelled of mercy ... scents of grace and love.

At first, as this Candle knelt in that blackness, it appeared as though it didn't want to be lit, as if there might be another way to chase away the darkness. Finally, the Candle allowed itself to be lit, and the flame burned. The Candle yielded to the flame. Darkness fled in that garden.

The Candle burned brighter with each passing hour of its life, until the last bit of the candlewick became just a glowing ember.... dying. On a cross, dying. With its last glowing moments declaring, "It is finished." The Candle had accomplished its purpose.

When all the candles are lit at night, the house looks wonderful. There's just something about candlelight which the artificial bulb can't match. The flame is alive, moving ever so slightly with the breeze.

Be a candle. Allow the Father to use you as a light in a dark world. Yield yourself to Him. You'll find yourself becoming a holy fragrance and a source of light in a dark world. Maybe, just maybe, someone else will see their way because you became a light.

"Let your light so shine before men, that they may see your good works, and glorify your Father in heaven." (Matthew 5:17 KJV)

3

The Bowl

We bought this old wooden bowl at an antique shop in an adjacent town. I love anything made of wood, so I was on board when Mary wanted to buy it. I'm intrigued when an object has character, and this bowl had it in spades. Relatively plain, there was nothing ornate about it, crafted for function over form, a workingman's (or woman's) bowl. It sits for the moment, as my wife loves to rearrange often, on a coffee table in our living room.

What caught my attention was the inner surface of the bowl. It had hundreds of tiny little scratches and grooves going in all directions, remnants of a life used for mixing countless batches of whatever, left by spoons and whisks from days past. Then there were the stains, darker than the wood itself, origin unknown, although I'm sure this bowl looked beautiful when it was new.

It began life as a block of wood in some woodworker's shop, carved, along with many others, by loving hands. The craftsman then put it on a showroom shelf or took it to a market with hopes someone would purchase it and put it to good use; the use intended.

You see, this bowl sitting on our coffee table is not fulfilling its intended use. To us it was a decorative object, sitting there looking good, adding character to the room. That's not what bowls are for. A bowl is meant to hold something, it's meant to feel the swishing of a whisk as someone makes mashed potatoes or wooden spoons tossing a salad. Then, to sit on a dining room table holding its master's creation until those around it dig in and spoon out its bounty. Bowls are not meant to sit empty and just look pretty.

Think of yourself as a bowl for just a moment. You started out as a block of wood. The Master Woodworker saw something in you, so He took you, and with loving, experienced hands, made you into the bowl you are. When He first carved you, you were new, without a mark. But you weren't created to sit on a shelf for long. It was the Master Woodworkers intention for you to be used and enjoyed, to serve.

I should warn you, the service intended will have its consequences. Others will scrape, nick, chip and whisk away your perfection, leaving you with scars and scratches from those who were a little rough with you. You'll be dropped by accident, dunked in dishwater and scrubbed with a scouring pad as others try to clean you up. It can be a rough life for a bowl, but that's what bowls are for.

If you ask an antique dealer what makes an antique valuable, many times they'll reply, "It's the patina." The wear and tear of daily use. All these things give you character. After all, it isn't about what you look like at the end of your life is it? It's about your character.

"For I am already being poured out as a drink offering, and the time for my departure is close. I have fought the good fight, I have finished the race, I have kept the faith. There is reserved for me a crown of righteousness, which the Lord, the righteous Judge, will give me on that day." (2 Tim. 4:6,8 NIV)

4

Peas

I hate peas! Well, maybe "hate" is a little too strong of a word, but I'm not a fan by any stretch of the imagination.

When I was little, my mom would set me in my high chair in the kitchen and feed me while she cooked. Occasionally she would try to feed me peas. I say *try* because my usual response was to spit them out ... all over the kitchen floor.

As I grew up and ventured out on my own, I no longer had to eat peas. Then I met and married my wife and we had two wonderful children. On occasion, my bride would cook peas. On the surface this didn't seem so bad, I was an adult and I could choose not to eat them. Au contraire, my bride, as a way of getting the children to eat their vegetables, would say, "Watch your father, he'll eat them." What was I to do? Eat my peas - that's what.

You see, peas really are good for you. I knew it was more important for the kids to eat their vegetables than it was for me to satisfy my tastes. They may not suit your *taste*, but they do have nutritional value.

Aren't we like that as Christians? I don't *like* the music. You don't *like* the preaching. We don't *like* this or that, even though it may have a benefit for another Christian. That Christian may be a babe in Christ whose only example for growth is you. They may need the "peas" you don't like in their lives.

Could it be time for us to occasionally, or maybe even more often, not be so concerned about our *tastes* as opposed to being concerned for the growth of the church. If I had done a Google search and discovered that peas were in fact *bad* for you, there might be justification for not eating them. But that's just not the case.

When it comes to your *tastes* in the Body of Christ … eat your peas.

"Do nothing out of selfish ambition or vain conceit. Rather, in humility value others above yourselves." (Philippians 2:3 NIV)

5

The Lake

We have a little lake in our neighborhood. When it's full, it's beautiful. As you crest a hill on the entry road, it's the first thing you see.

The past couple of years, it's been losing its water. You see, there is a breach in the levee at one end. Mountain streams trickle into it from above, but they can't seem to keep up with the water flowing out of the breach.

When the lake is full, it reflects the beauty of God's mountains surrounding it. It displays a mirror image of every wondrous cloud that floats gently over it. When full of water, the lake displays all of God's handiwork. But when the water gets too low, you can see the dead, haggard, twisted trees that began to grow the first time it drained. Ugly and tangled.

I spent the better part of a day with an axe and chainsaw out in that dried lake bed hacking and cutting down tree after tree. It was difficult work. Each ugly tree had to be cut and dragged out in a certain order, so I could get to the next tree. One at a time, they gave up their hold on the mud and weeds.

Oh, the weeds—I failed to mention them. Everywhere you looked, the dry bed was covered by a thick layer of weeds. They had reached up to entangle anything in their path. Eventually I hacked that entire stand of trees down. Tired and hot and thirsty, I turned around and was confronted with another stand of gnarled trees I hadn't seen from the road. "Never ending!" I said. "When will they stop?" The truth is, if the lake keeps leaking, they won't stop.

What's a follower of Christ to do? I mean, God fills us with His wondrous Word and His Holy Spirit. He wants us to reflect Him and everything He's created. He feeds us with streams of living water from His great mountain, flowing into us from the peaks of Heaven.

Then one day comes the breach. Small at first. Skipping a devotional time one day. Forgetting to pray the next day. Too busy to read His Word regularly. And so the breach widens, ever so slightly, bit by bit, until one day you look around and realize that you're losing water. Living water.

Eventually, if you're paying attention, you'll notice a weed, or a little tree begin to take root. So you may put your finger in the breach for a moment. When you can no longer see the trees or weeds growing in, you ease up on the breach and the water begins to flow out again. But the next time you see the trees and weeds they're ugly now, twisted and grotesque.

You see, trees are not meant to grow under water. Sin is not meant to grow under grace. Nothing ugly belongs in God's creation, so my axe became like the Word from God. My chainsaw became like prayers lifted to the Father, as tree by tree was cut down at its base. Oh, to be sure, the scars from the trees are still there, but they're no longer alive. They are dead. I know when God fills the lake up, the surface will once again reflect His glory.

The breach in the lake. Well, it's still there, and every man-made effort to fix it so far has failed. We may have to put up with little breaches in our lives, but you know what? Just keep looking toward the mountain, from whence cometh your water. He will supply endless streams that never dry up. Through the power of His Word and the filling of His Holy Spirit, you'll still reflect His glory.

"Create in me a pure heart, O God, and renew a steadfast spirit within me." (Psalm 51:10 NIV)

6

The Bow

One day my daughter told me she was interested in archery, so I signed her up for a lesson. Thinking of myself as an outdoorsy guy, I caught the bug.

Soon I was perusing archery forums and found I could make my own bow. How cool would that be? So, after researching, reading, and absorbing info, I set out to my local home improvement store to find a piece of wood.

The lumber available at these stores isn't ideal for bow making, but I decided I'd rather lose $7 learning than lose much more by investing in quality materials without knowing what I was doing. So, board in hand, I embarked on this journey of creation. In case you didn't know, they call a person who makes bows a *bowyer*. Cool, huh?

To create a bow, you first need to study wood grains, tree types, flex, brace height, draw length, weight, knock placement, string type, reflex, deflex, longbow, recurve...whew! I discovered this wasn't going to be as easy as I had first imagined. But I set out on developing my bowyer skills, sawing, sanding, filing, tillering (yeah, look that one up!), more sanding, filing, tillering...you get the picture.

After six or seven days of this, my piece of wood began taking shape. Next, I carved out a handle to fit my hand, and after many adjustments—fine tuning, as they call it—I put a bow string on it. When I held it up, it looked like a real bow. Well, a homemade bow, but a bow that I was proud of nonetheless.

Then came the ultimate test: would it fire an arrow across the back yard or snap in two, resulting in failure? With my cardboard box target all set up, I knocked, or loaded in layman's terms, an arrow and took aim, just as primitive people had done in days of old. I drew the arrow back and let it fly.

It missed the mark, ending up in the side of my wooden shed. More adjusting...and more...and more. To my amazement, this time the arrow hit the box! Man was I excited! I had taken a piece of wood and, through hard work and perseverance, turned it into something special.

That's my creation story. There's another creation story, and it's you and me. We are an amazing creation, aren't we? Our Heavenly Father took a raw natural material, the dust of the earth, and He created us. He scooped us up from the ground, shaped us into what He desired, a man and a woman, and put us in the garden.

Then one day, sin entered us, and we moved away from what our Creator intended. Instead of hitting the mark, we missed the target.

You might think His creation efforts were a complete failure by looking at society today. Thankfully, He doesn't believe that. One at a time, each of us has been beautifully crafted and lovingly put together just the way He wanted. He's still working on us, and one day, if we're His, we'll load our final arrow, let it fly, and go home to be with our Creator.

Remember that I talked about crafting a handle? Well, our Heavenly Father has crafted a handle in each of us that's custom made, not to fit us, but to fit His hand. When we put ourselves in His hands, the arrow always, always, hits its mark.

"Now it is God who makes both us and you stand firm in Christ. He anointed us, set his seal of ownership on us, and put his Spirit in our hearts as a deposit, guaranteeing what is to come." (2 Corinthians 1:22,23 NIV)

7

The Library

I love books. I'm somewhat of a collector. My wife came up with a rule not too long ago. When one book comes in, two books must go. If I bought a book, I needed to donate two. Her premise, I assumed, was for my collection to shrink, not grow.

My books were everywhere. Each little side table had one, or two, stacks piled on my desk where you could hardly see the desk itself. Living room, check. Bedroom, check. Den, double check! I had to do something to bring literary peace to the house.

So, I hatched a plan I felt would appease both of us. Simple in thought, not so simple in execution. I would build a bookcase. One of those floor-to-ceiling, take up a whole wall wonders of creation I'd only seen in Better Homes and Gardens. I believed, that if I built it, they would come. And when they came, they could stay. More room for books. Yeah.

So, it began, I built the behemoth. Seven and a half feet tall, twelve feet wide and thirteen inches deep. I believed it could hold every book I owned, all of Mary's and then some. I believed it would take a long time to *fill* up. I stood back in awe as Mary and my Mother in Law ooh'ed and aah'ed. Proud of my accomplishment, I secretly planned my first book hunt.

We, well actually Mary, loaded up the shelves and when it was all said and done, there wasn't that much room left. Where did all those books come from?

A little clarification is needed, I said I was an avid book *collector*, not a book *reader*. Yes, I love books, I simply have a hard time finishing them. In almost every book I own is a bookmark, left there when I put the book down the last time, often a long time ago. I guess my concentration level isn't what it used to be.

Some books are old because I love old books. Some have dust jackets, some are worn, others untouched. Big or small, they span a variety of subjects. Gardening. Theology. Classics. Books for each of my way-too- many hobbies, I said I had trouble with concentration.

Then one day I walked into the den and noticed that They all looked unfamiliar.

Something was different. Mary had taken all the dust jackets off of them, for you collectors out there she kept them safe. She also had arranged the books by the color of their spines. All the blues here, the blacks there, and every tonal variance in between. It *looked* awesome-it made being able to find a book almost impossible. But in time I adjusted. But I'm digress.

These books all have things in common. They all contain information. Information I thought, at one time, I wanted or needed. If I needed to know when to plant corn, I pulled out one of my gardening books. If I wanted to find out what a Bible verse meant, out came a commentary.

Each book had a purpose. They were either filled with pictures of faraway places I'd never been, with the power to take me there, or beautiful covers and grand illustrations pleasing to the eye. Still others tattered and worn from too much use. Many of them told stories I loved. Some books were meant to be read for simple enjoyment. A few, I'd hardly touched since bringing them into the family.

They were all different, but they were "my" library. In them I found comfort, I found help, I found joy. Some made me cry, others made me mad. Sometimes reading just a paragraph, other times an entire chapter, and on rare occasion an all-night, can't stop, page turner. Some I gave a cursory perusal and put on the shelf forever or gave away because I didn't need them anymore. They had outlasted their usefulness. Some I treasure but rarely pull off the shelf to read. In the end, all of them were a part of my library.

There's another library, and it's not mine, it's the Lord's. Yep. He built it starting with two books. One named Adam, and the other Eve. God's first two books. And He's been building this library since before the foundation of the world.

Each of us a book. Some of us an open book for the world to see and enjoy. Others, not so open, not ready to be perused. We weren't put on this earth to sit on a shelf and collect the dust of a life not used for its purpose. Each of us was made to be opened and read, looked at and questioned.

Sometimes God rearranges us, takes our dust jackets off. Exposes us. He places us next to books on a shelf we don't care for. But He can do that. He's the Librarian, He's the Publisher, and He's the Author of each of our lives. Every word, every sentence, paragraph and chapter of our lives are wonderfully, masterfully written.

There are people out there who need knowledge. They need joy and peace. They need to be able to come to us and *get away* from what they're going through. To know how we could cope.

Written on the pages of the lives of God's people are answers. Answers people need. Answers people want.

We are the great library God has created. We should be a place anybody can go to for what they need.

Not sit on a shelf. If you find yourself afraid, you can always go to God's written Word. I know I don't need to remind you that books have a front cover and a back cover. Just remember, when you open the front cover of God's Word, He's got your back.

Oh, and one final thought, the owner of the book writes their name *inside* the front cover to show it belongs to them. Others can't see who owns the book until it's opened. Be an open book, embrace the library.

"In the same way, let your light shine before others, that they may see your good deeds and glorify your Father in heaven." (Matthew 5:16 NIV)

8

The Spring

Spring has sprung here on Poplar Hill. Suddenly the grass is greener, and the peach trees display pretty pink flowers. Days are getting longer. Leafless mountainsides turn various shades of green in patches.

Life is emerging where it looked as if no life existed a month ago. Spring recalls a new life.

To be sure, there was life in the trees that appeared lifeless in the dead of winter. Daffodil bulbs still had breath in them even in the frozen ground. The beginnings of what I hoped to be peaches this year still sat deep inside the bare branches of the peach trees. The life in all of them patiently awaiting the right moment to move again.

Spring reminds me of patience. Something that, for me, never comes easy. When I want something, I want it now.

But I can't plant my Arkansas Traveler tomatoes in the frozen garden ground. And the roses by the front porch won't bloom in a snow-covered bed. I must wait. And that's okay. I need to understand that the winter preceding this time of renewing had an important purpose. Rest. Something that impatient people struggle with. God knew my garden ground needed a rest. The trees, flower bulbs, and peaches—they all needed time to rest.

You see, if we try to force our agenda on God, it never works. He may, in His infinite wisdom, keep us in the winter of our lives for a reason. Sometimes we need to rest. In Him. After all, He orders the seasons. In this grand universe that spans countless light years in any direction, it was He who ordered the spring to arrive at just the right moment here on Poplar Hill.

He also orders the spring right where you are. You may have come through a winter in your life where it seems as if nothing has been accomplished. If so, then step outside, walk a path, and sit on a porch and observe as God turns the life switch on again. If you're still in your winter, take a deep breath and have a little patience. Think of it as a time of rest and realize that spring always follows winter. He's been planning this spring forever. Your spring. Watch as God brings back to life the things you thought were dead.

"And out of the ground the Lord God made to spring up every tree that is pleasant to the sight and good for food." (Genesis 2:9. ESV)

9

The Mountain

For the last several years I've had a mild obsession with mountain climbing. At one time I even had an unrealistic hope of climbing Mount Everest. I know it was a long shot…but I could dream, couldn't I? When I realized that wasn't going to happen, I said maybe I can just hike to the Everest base camp. It's at 17,500 feet of elevation, so even that would be an accomplishment. Alas, my checkbook said no.

So, I've relegated myself to reading books about mountain climbing and hiking near home. After all, I live in the mountains of western North Carolina. I love the hiking. I've covered an incredible thirty-three miles of the Appalachian Trail, though not all at one time, and hiked five mountains over six thousand feet in our area.

I guess it's the challenge of the climb that fascinates me, and I've learned a thing or two about mountains along the way. You need to know yourself, your capabilities, and your condition before you attempt a climb. If your condition is not up to the mountain you've chosen, you have to either train more or choose an easier mountain. You also have to know the mountain, how steep it is, and how long the round trip is to the top and back. Once I do my calculations and believe I'm ready, I set out on the climb.

But I must tell you, there are always unexpected surprises. Rocks to climb over, fallen trees to hurdle, ledges to negotiate. Then those endless switchbacks that turn "a mile as the crow flies" into two or three. There are thistles, thorns, and brambles, none of which can be seen from the bottom of the mountain. You must climb to find out—to get on the mountain before it reveals its sometimes not-so-little secrets. Expect the unexpected with mountain climbing.

The unexpected isn't always something negative. How about the beauty of those views from the top of a mountain? Vast vistas of forest, snow caps, fall colors, and spring foliage. Maybe the opportunity to see for miles through clear air. Or a chance encounter with a doe along the path. The Eagles nest, the rhododendron, and the blackberry bush.

We face many mountains in our lives. Some of our own choosing, and some not expected. We should try to study them wisely. Can I climb this in my condition? Am I ready to tackle it, or do I need more training? Do I need to be better equipped?

In the end, mountain climbing requires faith. You must train, equip, study, and plan, but ultimately, with faith you take that first step. Everest climbers will tell you that each journey up the mountain is a little different. The weather, the terrain, and the environment are ever changing.

There is one major mountain we must all climb. The mountain of life. Ever changing, with surprises around every corner. You plan and prepare as best as you can, but there are always surprises. Some you're able to navigate easily and others are not so easy. But you go on—you must go on.

The folks who climb mountains, at least the ones who've attempted the big ones, all study the experiences of fellow mountaineers. They read each other's accounts of climbing and learn from each other's mistakes and successes. Some of them have even written mountain climbing manuals. Teaching guides that tell you how to climb, what equipment you'll need.

There is a manual for the mountain of life, and it's called God's Word. The Bible. God inspired folks like you and me to put in writing their journeys and experiences, so we could learn from their failures and successes, so He could communicate to us through them and help us along the path. Difficulties and challenges face us all.

Studying God's Word will help make your ascent easier and prepare you for the unexpected challenges of the climb…and no matter what difficulties you encounter, there will always be a rhododendron, blackberry bush, or deer to bring moments of joy along the way…then when you reach the summit, the view is Heaven as far as the eye can see.

"… come let us go up to the mountain of the Lord, to the House of the God of Jacob. He will teach us about His ways so we may walk in his paths." (Micah 4:2 ESV)

10

The Winter Night Sky

I love the night sky in the winter. Coming from a city where light pollution was a fact of life to a rural western North Carolina small town, the difference is striking. I can see so many more stars. The air is cleaner; it's a different world. Constellations seem to jump out at you. It's as if you can peer into heaven itself, each star being an angel. The winter night sky has a certain deep blackness to it that magnifies points of light. There truly is beauty in the darkness.

In what seems like direct opposition, all the trees and foliage seem to die in the winter here. Sometimes as I look around the neighborhood, it feels like I'm in a Sleepy Hollow movie set. Dark, tangled branches intertwined. Nothing green, all brown or gray, appearing lifeless. The few birds still around seem to flit from tree to tree, as if lost and looking for something. Everywhere I go, it's the same scene. It can be depressing.

But there are a few upsides to winter here. As you look out across the mountains, you can finally see the topography, the little valleys, gorges, and hollows you couldn't see before. And houses pop up, like little pockets of life, where you thought there was only wilderness. Smoke rises from chimneys you didn't even know were there. Old logging roads twisting their way up mountainsides appear out of nowhere.

Life is a seasonal thing and we all have winters to endure. Times where everything around us seems lifeless, dark, and cold. We look for brightness and warmth, but see only tangled branches surrounding us, with gray, overcast skies. All we want to do is retreat inside ourselves, close our eyes and dream of the coming spring. But I would challenge you to keep your eyes open. Peer through your tangled view, and you may just see little pockets of life where you thought none could be.

The Creator planned the winter as surely as the spring. The tangled leafless trees aren't dead.

They're sleeping…waiting for their Creator to say to the sap, "Rise and renew your host." Spring forth from the cold, frozen ground and rejuvenate. Winter is a time of rest for the mountains.

Could it be that you're in a winter so God can reveal an old logging road He wants you to travel that you wouldn't have seen through the foliage (read "busy times") of life? Maybe He's revealing a pocket of life He wants you to encounter for His purpose.

The next time it seems like a dark night in your life, embrace it. Go outside late at night, when it's the darkest. Look up! Be amazed at how your God can take the darkest of times and use them to reveal His beauty in the stars. You might be amazed at what He can show you in the winter night sky.

"I have come into the world as a light, so that no one who believes in me should stay in darkness." (John 12:46 NIV)

11

The Garden

I just broke ground for this year's garden. Covered over with weeds from the fall and winter's inactivity, it looked nothing like my garden. Unrecognizable except for the outline where the rabbit wire fence had been, a stake or two from last year's pole beans, and a tin pie plate lying on the ground beneath where it had once hung from a stick, clanging in the spring and summer breezes calling out to the crows, "Stay away from the corn!"

When I cranked up the tiller, it was hard to start after a winter's rest. Slowly it began to chug, then leveled off to a steady hum.

From the moment the first blade hit the dirt, things looked familiar. The North Carolina clay mixed with a truckload of Wayne's Feed Store's secret mixture came to life. Deep terra-cotta colored clumps rose with each rotation of the tiller's blades. This lifeless garden began its resurrection to new life.

Soon, with proper nurturing and attention, there would be lettuce, crispy sweet peppers, sweet corn, summer squash, cucumbers, and spinach competing for nutrients in this little patch of ground.

I love it when the first sign of a vegetable pops its head out of the soil. Signs of life let me know I've done something right. I'm rewarded for weeding, tending, watering, and fertilizing.

Sometimes life can be like my garden. There are cold, dark, cloudy seasons where we feel dormant, seemingly unrecognizable. We don't feel like the souls we were created to be, and on our own we sometimes feel powerless to change.

Then, at just the right time, we hear the hum of a heavenly tiller driven by the Master Gardener. As the tiller's blades bite into our outer shell of weeds, rocks, and sticks, it hurts at first. Roots have set in. Roots of despair, distrust, and disobedience. Sins we've allowed to take hold are sometimes hard to yield to the Gardner.

Then, when the tilling's done, the Master Gardner kneels to our level and plucks each weed, picks up each stick, and throws each rock out of the garden.

It gets easier to let go because the soil trusts that the Gardner is doing the right thing. When He's done, we are free from the obstacles of our growth.

Now! Yes, now it's time. The season's right, the moon's right, the weather's right, as everything the Master Gardener has been doing culminates in that moment when He places a seed in us. Sometimes He lets us select the seed. Sometimes He surprises us by offering a seed we didn't expect. He knows He can now trust us with what He has for us.

And He sows—seeds of sweet mercy, seeds of forgiveness, of helping others more than ourselves. Seeds of giving and seeds of joy. A wonderful garden created to supply our families, our churches, and our neighborhoods with all that they need.

If we yield ourselves completely to the Master Gardener, He will even tend us. He'll continue to weed us, and at just the right time, He'll bring fertilizer to help us produce better and become stronger.

You see, the garden wasn't meant to feed itself, to grow for itself, or to supply itself. The Master Gardener creates a garden only so that others may enjoy its bounty, benefiting from it by being fed. That's what a garden is for. You were meant to be His garden. Yes, underneath all your weeds, sticks, and rocks is a garden, waiting for the Master Gardener.

"For we are His workmanship, created in Christ Jesus for good works, which God prepared beforehand that we should walk in them." (Ephesians 2:10 ESV)

12

See the Shot

I love golf. I don't play well; in fact, it's been quite a while since I swung a club. But sometimes on weekends I sit in my recliner and watch tournaments, wishing I was there. I'm particularly enamored by the spectacle of The Masters in Augusta and The British Open in Great Britain, with their beautiful scenery.

One thing I've noticed among the better golfers is this: they step up to the ball, take a few practice swings, then step back behind the ball facing their target, and occasionally you can see them close their eyes. Maybe it's only for a moment or two, but they do it.

What they're doing is visualizing the shot. In their mind they address the ball, concentrate, swing, and try to see the shot happen in their mind. They mentally follow the ball as it leaves the earth, soaring along the path intended, landing on the fairway or green in the exact spot where the golfer wanted it to land. It's amazing how all of that happens in just a few seconds.

Sports psychologists have been teaching visualization for some time. It's nothing new. "See the shot," they say. Close your eyes and ignore all the distractions.

For a marathon runner, it's *imagining* themselves crossing the finish line in record time. Great quarterbacks can *visualize* where their receiver will be before they even make the inside cut or buttonhook. Baseball players can *predict* which pitch is coming because of the count and the pitcher's delivery.

Even in everyday life, at least for me, I prefer to be shown how to do something. There's an amazing motivation in each of us that likes to see what's coming.

I'm glad The Holy Spirit is our spiritual sports psychologist. Teaching us how to succeed. If we rely on him, He will give us clues of what's in store for us. In fact, He uses a training manual that has a lot of visualization already done for us. The Word of God. We simply need to read it and trust that the author knows the future.

Read Revelations 5:9-13, Revelations 21:4, and Revelations 22:1-5, when you have some quiet time. Then simply close your eyes and visualize how grand Heaven will be. The goal is to be where Jesus is, and if you're a Christian, you'll be able to *see* yourself there. One day, you'll open your eyes for the last time. You'll discover that you've left the earth, traveled along the path you and God intended, and landed exactly where you wanted.

"And if I go and prepare a place for you, I will come back and take you to be with me that you also may be where I am." (John 14:3 NIV)

13

Eb and Flo

Remember the old "Chicken Little" syndrome? While the sky may not be falling, there sure has been a lot of negative stuff happening in the world. Throughout history there have been troubled times that would make anyone think there is no hope. If you were a Jew and a crazy dictator was rounding up about six million of your friends, or if you were down to your last loaf of bread during the Great Depression, or maybe even huddled in a farmhouse basement watching a few thousand other Americans march toward you with cannons and long rifles, you could say things were bleak. But, to date, the end of the world has yet to come.

Let me introduce you to an interesting couple. They've been together for 70 years, which is an amazing accomplishment because their personalities could not be more opposite.

At 92 years old, she's seen her share of hard times. Somehow, she always seems to find a way to make ends meet, to get something out of nothing. She can take a simple potato and make it taste like a four course, five-star meal. Watch as she pulls together some pieces of worn out cloth and suddenly, she's made a colorful Christmas scarf. Notice her smooth ability to sweet talk the electric company into waiting just another couple of days before they turn off the juice. There is a peace about her. Her name is Flo, and for her age, she looks darn good.

Eb on the other hand, has perfected the art of imperfection. He's only 87, but in that time, he's figured out how to make a rainbow break a promise, and how to see a smiley face as only a yellow dot. For him, five gallons of gas only goes a mile. He has that "I've got a lot of miles on me" look.

But they've spent so much time together that they know each other's thoughts. They've learned to live with each other. He knows she will always come through. She knows he's not as bad as all that. She's figured out how to *not* let him throw her off her game. Even a bad day only lasts twenty-four hours, and a week is only seven days long.

Yes, there are a lot of bad things happening in the world. There is much uncertainty around every corner. If you let your mind succumb to negative things, they can take years off your life. You can choose to see either a half-full glass, or a half-empty one.

For the follower of Christ, there is only hope. If the world as we know it ends, we'll have a brand-new home. That's why so many believers can face death with peace. Even with a smile. Read the accompanying verse and, when you're standing on the seawall watching your world wash away, and the tide seems to be "Eb-bing," go with the Flo.

"For I know the plans I have for you, declares the Lord, plans to prosper you and not to harm you, plans to give you a hope and a future." (Jeremiah 29:11 NIV)

14

The Orchestra

Have you ever experienced an orchestra? I remember Mary and I going to see Les Misérables some time ago. In front of the stage was a large pit, the orchestra pit. As I looked over the edge I could see all the instruments, waiting on their respective players.

The layout also fascinated me. Every section, and every instrument in every section, was in its designated place. I mean, who would dare place the intimate flute right next to the mighty tuba? It was like looking at a musical map where each instrument had just the right amount of space around it. The tympani, harp and percussion had the most. The cello, viola and trombone had ample space. The trumpet placed so as not to play to close to the ear sitting in front. It was amazing.

Then there's the conductor. I have always been fascinated by the conductor of an orchestra. They have this big, music score laid out in front with every note, rest, time signature, when to get loud, when to get soft, all written out. And yet the conductor rarely ever seems to look at the music. The conductor's eye seems to be darting back and forth from cello, to bassist. From first violin to piccolo. Brass to woodwinds, always a step ahead, always knowing who should come in and when ... and how. It's art in motion.

Did you also notice the conductor's always elevated on a platform above the orchestra? Not below, or even with, but above. That's for a reason. If the conductor were below, then those in the middle and rear could not see, and wouldn't know when to come in. If the conductor were even with the orchestra, they could barely see the baton as it darted back and forth, up and down. The conductor is above so everyone can see them.

I'm convinced that the conductor is the key here. You could be the most amazing first violinist, but unless the conductor directs you, you won't fit into the grand theme of the music. You may come in a tad too soon and become the solo that was never written.

The conductor knows the music, backwards and forwards, inside and out. Every note, every section, every staff, key change, the conductor knows it all.

It's imperative, if you want to be in the conductor's orchestra, that you be a team player. If you watch, even the most famous guest violinists, such as Itzhak Perlman, know when to shine. They know when to blend in, and when to take a back seat to another instrumentalist. All because of the conductor.

There is an unspoken trust between the conductor and the orchestra. You be ready, trained, polished, practiced...and I'll tell you when to come in so that the music we make together is as written. I won't bring you in early and embarrass you, or ask you to play someone else's part, for which you weren't created. I won't hold you back when it's your turn to shine. I'll bring you in at the exact time designed for your part.

Where do you fit in the Great Conductor's orchestra? If you're a *follower* of Jesus Christ, you are in the orchestra. And God has given you an instrument. It was a gift, customized with you in mind. You may have the gift of encouragement or the gift of teaching. Some of you have the gift of service, others the gift of prophecy. But *all* of us have at least one instrument to play in the grand orchestra of life.

The Great Conductor wants us to practice, polish, learn, practice more, and then be watching and ready for when He brings us in. We don't get to play every note. We don't get a solo every time. But we get to come in at just the right time and play a role in the score of the Great Conductor. Are you ready? Have you even tried to learn what instrument He wants you to play? There are many musicians running around the world who are playing the wrong instrument. Why don't you pray the Great Conductor of eternity show you which instrument you need to be, and He will use you in the orchestra of life...
... that would be eternal life.

"**Praise him with the sounding of the trumpet, praise him with the harp and lyre, praise him with timbrel and dancing, praise him with strings and pipe, praise him with the clash of cymbals, praise him with resounding cymbals. Let everything that has breath praise the Lord.**" (Psalm 3-6 NIV)

15

Beautiful Noise

O nce again spring reveals another round of green grasses, budding trees and gorgeous flowers. Fresh rains wash pollen from the air, squirrels dance and scamper, rabbits hop, and the birds, oh those birds. Cardinals, Blue Jays, Robins, Finches and the occasional Pileated Woodpecker all competing for the ear of the listener.

Taking the dogs out in the morning has become my favorite time. It's as if the volume and variety of bird sounds reach a musical crescendo as the sun rises over the horizon. Each warble, chirp, whistle and song unique to its species, all singing in a wonderful avian concerto. It truly is a beautiful noise.

Why is it, even with all the different species competing for the same auditory space, that it is still such a beautiful noise? Maybe because the different species each have the same purpose, to praise the rising of the sun. To accompany the newness of the morning with song.

The church could take a lesson from these little creatures. Each of us with our individual beliefs, preferences, wants, demands and have-to's, all raising our voices clamoring to be heard. The music we like, the mission we prefer, that preacher, this order of worship, all based on us.

When there is unity of purpose and of focus, we see something amazing happen. In the musical world it's called *harmony*. The wonderful thing about harmony is, it doesn't require every note to be the same. In fact, you can't have harmony when every note is the same.

What it requires is that each note plays its designated role. Whether a soprano, tenor, alto or bass, each is placed where they will sound the most pleasing. Each placed in its proper position by the arranger, the creator. Each told where to come in on which note by the conductor. Point being, each note is not in charge. Each voice does not chart its own course. It responds to the choir director. To the conductor.

Each Easter, Christians celebrated the rising of our Savior Jesus Christ. Many of us have sunrise services. We, like the birds, lift our voices at our different places, singing praise to the *Son* as the sun rose. Together, in harmony, all with one thing in mind. Praising a risen Lord. One focus. You need not be a cookie cutter Christian, in fact, that's not what harmony is about. But working together with the purpose of creating the chord that the Conductor desires is. When the church, like the birds, begins their day by raising their voices in praise to a risen Son, then it truly is a beautiful noise.

"My mouth will speak in praise of the Lord. Let every creature on earth bless his holy name for ever and ever." (Psalm 145:21)

16

Time

I'm obsessed with time. More accurately, I'm obsessed with collecting time, in the form of watches and antique clocks. Dive watches, tough watches, watches worn in movies, and space-related watches.

I discovered this little app for my phone that checks the accuracy of my watches. When it tells you, you hit this little button, and then twelve hours later you hit the little button again and it tells you how many seconds per day your watch is ahead or behind.

But wait, ahead or behind what? Ahead or behind what's known as the Atomic Clock. When I looked up what an atomic clock was it said, "a clock device that uses an electron transition frequency in the microwave, optical, or ultraviolet region of the electromagnetic spectrum of atoms as a frequency standard for its timekeeping standard." Excuse me...did any of you understand that? It's way, way above my head! All I wanted to know was what time it was.

Time is important. It tells me when I need to be somewhere. It tells me how long I have until payday, when my birthday party is going to begin, or how long I have before that boring show is over. I use time to cook, work, play and sleep. Time measures so much of our lives.

From the Bible's perspective, time is important too. The Psalmist David said, "How long oh Lord? Will you forget me forever? How long will you hide your face from me?" How about the prophet Habakkuk: "How long, LORD, must I call for help...?" Jesus told Peter and the disciples to "... stay in the city until you are clothed with power from on high." Even as Christians consider when the Lord is coming back, we're told not until we hear the great trumpet sound.

Time affects so much of our lives. Maybe that's why I love collecting timekeepers. I even have an antique mantle clock from the mid 1800's over my fireplace so I can listen to a chime someone else listened to during Civil War days.

I've come to learn that no matter how hard I try to get to an appointment early, or how much I wish that last wonderful vacation day would never end, I can't stop time.

Maybe Jesus had it right after all, when describing the end times. He said, "But concerning that day and hour no one knows, not even the Angels of heaven, nor the Son, but the Father only."

Our concern shouldn't be about time. We can't stop time. We can't slow it down or speed it up. Maybe we should just leave this whole time thing up to the only one who controls it, and it's not the Atomic Clock, it's the Lord.

"He changes times and seasons; he deposes kings and raises up others. He gives wisdom to the wise and knowledge to the discerning." (Daniel 2:21 NIV)

17

New Fallen Snow

One of my favorite pastimes is sitting on my carport swing in the dead of winter right after an overnight snow. There's just something magical about it. When I go to bed, it is dark and cold outside, and everything looks dead. The trees are bare; the grass has turned mottled shades of brown; nature appears lifeless.

When my alarm goes off early in the morning, I roll out of bed. I feed the dog and toast a slice of raisin bread, grab my java, open the living room blinds, and voila! A bright white landscape, pristine and pure, is spread before my eyes. The amazing beauty always strikes me as though something has transformed the world outside my window into the adage, *a winter wonderland*.

Bundled up and warm, coffee cup in hand, sitting on my swing, I notice a few things while surveying the landscape. It's always the most beautiful when it's new snow. It hasn't fallen from the pine boughs yet, there are no footprints left by man or beast, and you can't see the mud that will surface once cars make their way down your dirt road.

Everything's brighter as the sun reflects off the new-fallen ground cover. Untouched! Yes, that's the word I was looking for. What the good Lord sent down from the sky is untouched by human hands.

Then the first morning pickup truck rumbles down the path leaving two deep, track-like scars. Your neighbor steps outside and walks his three dogs, one of which takes a spin across your yard as you wave hello. Little by little, what had been pristine and untouched shows signs left by a human upon God's creation, detracting from the original glory of the morning.

When it comes to our lives in Christ, we can take a lesson or two from what God does overnight with a snowfall. When you become a Christian something amazing happens. God forgives your sins. Scriptures tell us old things pass away, and you become a new creation, just like the freshly fallen snow.

But then your feet leave behind tracks, having been places they shouldn't have walked. Your hands knock the snow from the limbs, uncovering old dead branches by touching things they shouldn't have touched. Suddenly, your pristine and clean appearance takes a turn, and it isn't for the better. You no longer look like a new creation anymore; you look like the old version before the snow fell. Will you ever see newness again?

Take heart, my friend, there's hope in Christ. The same Scriptures tell us that one day, instead of a pristine covering of snow that falls, you and I will rise in glory, created anew, and we'll join those saints who've gone before us around the throne and, like them, we'll be wearing pure white raiment, only this time we'll be whiter than the new-fallen snow.

"Cleanse me with hyssop, and I will be clean; wash me, and I will be whiter than snow." (Psalm 51:7 NIV)

18

Little Plastic Cup

In a Sunday evening service at the church I attend, we were about to take part in the Lord's Supper. As they were getting ready to pass out the juice, which represents the blood of Christ, I sat in quiet contemplation.

A myriad of thoughts raced through my head: Was I worthy? Was there any sin I'd forgotten to confess? Had I been good enough to partake?

You know, the way we look at ourselves plays a large role in how we feel. If we see ourselves as unworthy or unclean, that perception can affect us. If we don't like what we see, our self-image can steal our joy, bring us sadness, or even throw us into depression. I don't believe it is God's intent for us to feel that way.

Most of the time, a negative self-concept comes from sin. Not just what you may have done or not done, but the overall sin condition of mankind. Makes you want to say, "Thanks Adam!!" now and then.

But we're all responsible, which reveals one of the greatest truths in the Bible. God sent His only Son Jesus to be a sacrifice for our sins. Adam's sin, mine, and yes, even yours. I'm glad Jesus's shed blood covered my sins.

As I sat there holding that little plastic cup of juice between my thumb and forefinger, my middle finger was resting underneath the cup. The evening sun was still streaming through the windows, and a couple of rays were illuminating the red grape juice.

Cradling that cup, I realized, when I looked at the juice, that I couldn't see the finger that was underneath the cup. All I could see was the juice. I couldn't see the scar on my finger from a burn I'd received many years before; I couldn't see the wear and tear from working in the garden; I couldn't see that finger at all.

When we're covered by His blood, we are covered by His blood. He no longer sees our sin because we're forgiven. It's Satan who likes to remind us of those things and hopes we'll continue to dwell on them instead of God's great love for us.

The next time you're feeling down, sad, or depressed about who you think you are or what you've done or not done, think of that little plastic cup of juice. He's got you covered!

"In him we have redemption through his blood, the forgiveness of sins, in accordance with the riches of God's grace." (Ephesians 1:7 NIV)

19

For or With

Sometimes revelations can be inspiring. You know, those *aha* moments when we realize something new. Sometimes revelation can be painful, like one of those, "the truth hurts," moments.

As I grow older I realize, like most of us, that I've wasted a lot of time in my life. Things left unfinished, pursuits left unattained, goals not achieved. The operative words in those statements are *unfinished, unattained,* and *not achieved.* Each of those words suggest *my* attempting something and failing.

Applied to my spiritual life, these words are unsettling. Each statement also begins with words like *thing, pursuits,* and *goals.* While Jesus does ask His followers to do things for Him, such as the great commission, and He does ask His followers to treat each other in certain ways, we must always be cognizant of the first thing He ever asked His followers to do.

Matthew 4:19 Jesus gives His first instructions, "Follow me and I will make..." What or where doesn't matter. What matters is who. Our first responsibility is to "Follow" and our second is to let Him "make". The more *we* try to do *for* Him the more things can get muddled up.

Try this little exercise. On a sheet of paper, in two columns side by side, write down things you have done *for* Jesus, like; taught a bible study, tithed, volunteered, attended church and such. In the other column, write down how much time you have spent *with* Jesus ... on your knees in prayer, reading His Word *with* Him and listening *to* Him.

Hang on, it gets harder, now try this. If you're reading this and you've ever been in love with someone, remember back when you were dating? You might go to the movies, or out to eat, but if you're honest, *where* you went and *what* you did probably wasn't as important as *who* you were with. Doing *things* without Jesus, even though they're nice things, is still doing *things* without Jesus. His first words to you every morning when you wake up are, "Come, follow me, and I will make..." The rest is up to Him, not you.

"Let the morning bring me word of your unfailing love, for I have put my trust in you.
Show me the way I should go, for to you I entrust my life." (Psalm 143:8 NIV)

20

Indiana Corn

My wife's relatives come from a midwestern farming community where corn is one of the major crops. We traveled there recently for a family reunion. As we got nearer to our destination the landscape changed, and all we saw for miles were fields filled with eight-foot-tall deep green corn stalks waiting to bring forth their golden ears.

Splitting these fields, as if God's checkerboard, were dirt roads placed so they ran exactly north to south or east to west. I'm told by the locals you can set your compass by those roads, and that's not by accident. You see, the machinery my wife's family uses in today's modern times is usually controlled by a Global Positioning System, or GPS. You enter your coordinates for the day's work location into the on-board computer system built into a massive piece of farming equipment, press a button, and off you go. It's all ingenious as your vehicle takes you right up to the edge of a road that is perfectly aligned north to south, or east to west.

My wife's cousin took us to the family's farm equipment storage facility one day. As I entered the building, the enormous size of the equipment struck me. The tires on the John Deere combine were taller than me. Their planter plants 24 rows of seed one at a time, and they use a sprayer with a 120-foot boom for laying down fertilizer or pest control. Seeders, box drills, ginormous tractors, it all boggled my mind. I felt like an ant looking up at a set of Tonka Toys.

While my mind was swimming in all this amazing technology with its complicated systems, I stepped outside of the building for a breath of fresh Indiana air. I walked over to a row of corn stalks nearby and ran my fingers along the long leaves of one, smelling the tassel that was telling me the ears were coming soon. It was awe-inspiring.

With the tour over, we headed back to one cousin's house for a family cookout. Several generations circled the long dining room table and our host had us join hands while he gave thanks to the Lord for the bounty set before us.

That's when it hit me! Even with all the 21st century technology, expensive equipment, and long hours of labor, our host was still thanking the One who made it all possible, our Creator God. That million-dollar piece of equipment couldn't make a corn kernel sprout, then shoot up to around 8 feet tall, bearing ears of corn sweeter than rock candy. It was the land and the seed, the part God had created, that brought forth the bounty.

Growing corn takes long hours of hard work and dogged determination, but these folks recognized that it was God who gave the harvest.

"He makes the grass grow for the cattle, and plants for people to cultivate—bringing forth food from the earth." (Psalm 104:14 NIV)

21

Fast Food

Why is it we're willing to sit in *long* lines waiting on *fast* food? It's a bit of an oxymoron, isn't it? We tell ourselves we're in a hurry and getting food this way will help us get to wherever we're going faster, but do we? And while there has been a trend toward healthier choices, fast food doesn't tend to be the healthiest diet. Burgers, fries, chicken tenders, sodas, sweet tea (I hate to add that one) and such don't always fit into the five food groups we learned about in school.

Sometimes we treat God's word like fast food. We get in a hurry to go from point A to point B, and even though we need God's word as sustenance, we don't want to be late. As a result, we throw down a couple of verses, peruse a short Psalm, nod our head in a quick prayer, grab our keys, and out the door we go.

Let's take this analogy to a basic level. Food provides sustenance. We need food to live. If we don't eat, after a while the lack of nourishment will have a negative impact on our lives. Missing vitamins and nutrients will show up in our doctor's reports as reasons for failing health.

God's Word provides spiritual sustenance. We need it to live out our faith. If we don't study it, after a while, the lack of nourishment will begin to affect our lives. Missing time in God's Word, not meditating or praying over it, will show up on the spiritual report card of our lives as a reason for our lack of faith.

In God's Word we find comfort, strength, joy, peace, and all the other fruits of the Spirit. Each of these are spiritual nutrients God knows we need. Fear, uncertainty, worry, and a lack of peace in our lives result from not getting the right spiritual food. Look around to make sure no cars are coming, carefully pull out of the fast food line, and go get a home-cooked meal by spending time in His Word. It's free, it's on Him.

"Your words were found, and I ate them, and Your words became to me a joy and the delight of my heart, for I am called by Your name, O Lord, God of hosts." (Jeremiah 15:16 ESV)

22

The Cardinal

My son told me he'd found a baby bird in the backyard. When I first laid eyes on it, it was so small, eyes barely open. It appeared it had left the nest a tad before it was ready. And there it sat, on the ground in our backyard, all alone, looking tiny and helpless. We could not find the nest and saw no parents among the birds that frequent our yard.

That's when my son began regularly watching out for this little bird. He would check on it, watching it from our carport. I had almost resigned to the "let nature take its course" attitude figuring one day soon the little bird would succumb to the dangers it faced. I mean, after all, we live in the "mountains" and the life cycle is ever around us. My son told me he believed it was a baby female cardinal, and he'd seen what he thought were the parents among the trees.

Without realizing it, I got caught up in the "baby watch". I'd watch her flap her wings and sort of fly for maybe ten feet or so, low to the ground. As a "glass is half empty" fella, I feared the worse for our new little friend. She sat in the grass all day, among the ants, snakes, cats, and all sorts of other things I just knew would get her.

But, each evening and morning I would go out and she would be there, either curled up sleeping with her head facing backwards (how do they do that?) or bobbing her head looking around yawning.

One day as evening set, I slid an outdoor chair to one end of the carport where I could see her, but she couldn't see me. I settled in to watch her for a while, sitting real still, so as not to frighten the parents. Sure enough, not long after I sat down, I saw a beautiful crimson flash in the apple tree above her. Man was he gorgeous. This had to be the dad. I grabbed my binoculars and focused in. In his beak was a huge, green worm. Huge. He cautiously looked back and forth, then hopped down to the ground about two or three feet from our little girl.

As he approached her with supper, she appeared to ignore her father, and, in a moment, he flew off and disappeared into the surrounding foliage. A little later, he would repeat the same scene. And she would seem to ignore her father again. This time it took longer for him to return. But, after some fatherly coaxing with his beak his persistence paid off. She took the worm and ate. All the while it appears mother was watching from a nearby tree.

Well, after seeing this, I felt assured she was being well taken care of and my concern eased. This little scene played out for a couple of days.

Then one Sunday morning I got up, took the dogs out, but I didn't see our little girl. I distinctly remembered the spot I last saw her from the evening before, but she was nowhere to be found. I mean, she was small and could sit still and hide in the grass. So, I got my morning cup o' joe and went back outside and began a grid search of the backyard. Walk two feet and scan. Walk two feet and scan. Across the yard I went. Nothing. No feathers (thank the Lord!), nothing. I thought I could hear dad's calling but couldn't be sure.

Then, I heard a flapping next to me. I turned and couldn't believe my eyes. There, about four feet up in the apple tree, was our girl. Sitting on a limb stretching and yawning, apparently startled when I got too close. As I backed away she flew in a little circle and landed back on the ground. Dad fluttered from the aluminum roof of my shed, not happy with me being there. He met her on the ground and then flew back into the trees. I settle into my chair and watched. In a few minutes he was there again. Huge green worm and all. He flew to her and tried to feed her. At first, she ignored him, and I thought he would fly off, but not this time. After his first attempt, I mean it was a big worm, he adjusted the worm in his beak, so it would fit in her mouth and she gobbled it down. Breakfast had been served. Off he went, disappearing once again into the surrounding trees where I caught a glimpse of mother.

What a fascinating experience this had been. We thought this little helpless baby was a goner. No way she would survive living on the ground. She had fledged too early. Mom and dad couldn't put her back in the safety of the nest. She was exposed to all of her surroundings, good and bad. She faced danger at every turn. Crows, cats, dogs, ants, snakes (I said we lived in the woods, didn't I?) the possibility of thunderstorms in the forecast. But she didn't seem to care. She took each moment as it was given and made the best of each situation.

Then there was her father. Big, powerful looking, a wonderful bright crimson red, always watching but rarely seen, just close enough to save the day if needed. Bringing sustenance to her, but not forcing himself on her. Not "making" her eat. Patiently returning until she realized she needed the supper he was providing.

You know God is a lot like that father cardinal, don't you? After all, aren't we His creation? And doesn't He try to feed us? But He does not "force" himself upon us. We can accept His gifts, or not. To take the nourishment He offers or ignore it. And what He's offering is good for us. It is meant to sustain us, to give us life. If He is your Father, you can rest assured that He is watching over you.

You may not see Him, nor see His presence. You may think you're all alone among a whole slew of dangers, but He's there, always watching. I also noticed that when our little girl would call out, even a little peep, her father would answer. Back and forth they would communicate. He always answered. Sometimes not right away, but always.

One morning I saw the little girl sitting peacefully on the ground. Out of nowhere a blue jay swooped down and tried to attack the little cardinal. I was unprepared for this and didn't even know this type of thing happened. But something amazing followed. As soon as the blue jay swooped towards her, what seemed like every cardinal in the neighborhood came out of the surrounding trees and ran this jay off. Twice. And for a good hour after, all you saw was one after the other checking on our little girl. I never even knew that many cardinals were in the neighborhood. At least four males and three females. And the father stayed close the rest of the day.

Our Heavenly Father is the same way. Nothing happens to us He doesn't see. And He has the power to call down as many angels as is needed to protect you from your attacker. He's always watching. Waiting patiently to respond to any peep. Watching for danger all the time. Our little girl flew off into the woods. We haven't seen her in a few days. But I'm not worried. I've seen her Father. She's safe.

"My Father, who has given them to me, is greater than all; no one can snatch them out of my Father's hand." (John 10:29 NIV)

23

Hand Crafted

If you're at all like me, you appreciate quality. I love things that are hand-crafted. They evoke a time when we didn't have modern machines to do all the work for us. A time when people had skills. Sure, it was more demanding, more difficult, for someone to hand carve a wooden salad spoon, but they designed that spoon to last a lifetime. Nowadays we have throwaway stuff. It's cheaper to just buy another item.

If you talk to a craftsman, one of the reasons they'll give for making things the way they do is they love working with their hands. The carpenter loves to feel the grain of the wood, the weaver to run his hands through the wool, or the potter watching the clay squeeze through her fingers as she kneads it before putting it on the wheel.

In Genesis, the biblical account of God creating the world as we know it, something interesting happens.

He begins by creating the earth, the stars, the sun and moon, all the animals and birds. He does this by speaking. "And God said…" let there be light, let there be water, let there be this and that. With God, I must agree that His spoken word is powerful.

That's when something amazing occurs. God comes to what I consider the pinnacle of His creation, you… and me. When God creates man, the way I see it, He takes a more *intimate* approach. The Bible says He, "formed man from the dust of the ground…" I can picture God reaching down with His hands and grasping dust to hand-craft Adam.

Then the Scriptures say God "breathed into his nostrils the breath of life..." God's own breath of life. You and I have His breath in us. Later, these same scriptures will tell us that God took a rib from Adam and made Eve. He put Adam to sleep and did a little hands-on surgery. And when He finished hand-crafting you and I, He stepped back (I know I'm reaching a little here.) and said something He'd not said about any other part of His wonderful creation. He said, "It is *very* good."

Just like the craftsman who steps back and looks at their creation with the satisfaction they've made something special, by hand. When it comes to, (insert your name here), "... is very good."

"Then the Lord God formed a man from the dust of the ground and breathed into his nostrils the breath of life, and the man became a living being."
(Genesis 2:7 NIV)

Outro

I know … outro is a musical term for the "exit" from a piece of music, not literature. It's the opposite of intro. I just wanted to take a moment, now that you've finished this first work of mine to say thanks. There are so many literary works out there you could have chosen, but for some reason, you chose mine and I want to say thanks. Keep your eyes peeled and hopefully it won't be too long before the next *Random Encouragements* springs forth. God is always working, always revealing, always sharing.

Blessings

S E Hatfield

CPSIA information can be obtained
at www.ICGtesting.com
Printed in the USA
BVHW031340021118
531609BV00048B/425/P